W9-BZU-203

Everything You Need to Know About

LIVING WITH A GRANDPARENT OR OTHER RELATIVE

Today more and more grandparents are helping to raise their children's children.

• THE NEED TO KNOW LIBRARY •

Everything You Need to Know About

LIVING WITH A GRANDPARENT OR OTHER RELATIVE

Carolyn Simpson

THE ROSEN PUBLISHING GROUP, INC.
NEW YORK

Published in 1995 by The Rosen Publishing Group, Inc.
29 East 21st Street, New York, NY 10010

Copyright 1995 by The Rosen Publishing Group, Inc.

First Edition

Manufactured in the United States of America

Library of Congress Cataloging-in-Publication Data

Simpson, Carolyn.
    Everything you need to know about living with a grandparent or
other relative / Carolyn Simpson.
      p. cm. — (The need to know library)
    Includes bibliographical references and index.
    ISBN 0-8239-1872-6
    1. Grandparent and child—Juvenile literature. 2. Helping
behavior—Juvenile literature. 3. Intergenerational relations—
Juvenile literature. I. Title. II. Series.
HQ759.9.S57 1995
306.874′5—dc20
                                                         94-21291
                                                                  CIP
                                                                  AC

Contents

Once grandparents helped take care of their grandchildren. Today, it is almost common to find grandparents the sole caretakers of their grandchildren.

Chapter 1

What's Happening to Families Today?

Families have changed. In the past, two married parents raised their children. Sometimes grandparents lived with them, or nearby, and helped take care of the children. Nowadays, grandparents (and other relatives) are actually stepping in and raising these children themselves. What happened to the parents? What's been happening to our society?

Jon knew that his mother needed to go back to the hospital. She wasn't sleeping much at night, and she talked about being a movie star. She hardly had time to eat. He knew what was coming next. The crazy thoughts. The strange men she'd bring home. The checks she'd bounce.

So it didn't surprise him when Aunt Paula called him at school one day. "We've had to take your mom to the hospital," she said.

*"I guess that means I'm staying with you guys,"
Jon said, knowing the routine.*

*"It'll be okay," his aunt said. "We can get your
things this afternoon and check on the house. I'll
pick you up at three."*

*Jon didn't mind moving in with his aunt for a
while. At least it was predictable. Aunt Paula acted
like a regular person. She slept at night; she didn't
seem to get bad moods, and if she did, she never took
them out on him. Sure, he knew Mom had an ill-
ness. Something was chemically wrong with her
brain, the doctors said. But it was hard living in a
place where you didn't always feel safe. He was almost relieved now. At least, he had Aunt Paula and
Uncle Rick.*

Changes in the Family

Many people speak these days about the loss of
family values and the break-up of the "traditional"
family unit. Maybe life was simpler in an earlier
era. Or perhaps people always had problems
within the family that no one spoke about. There
is much discussion about this issue. No one is
certain of the answer. There is, perhaps, no
current agreed-upon norm as to what makes a
family. "Nontraditional families" can be dynamic
and exciting places of creativity and nurturing.
"Traditional families" can be places of deep
dysfunction. Whatever the nature of the family

Drug and alcohol abuse have had an even more profoundly negative impact on families in recent years.

unit, the family breaks down when children are not getting what they need, especially when there is abuse or neglect.

According to a recent survey, more than one million men are in prison today. When parents are in prison, they are not earning a living for their families. Some people believe that crime goes hand in hand with poverty, and that may well be true. Criminal behavior must be punished, however, and when it is, the result is that there is one less person earning an income to support his or her family.

Drugs are also changing the family. In the 1960s and '70s, heroin was the addictive drug of choice. But despite its horrors, families were often able to hold together because it was mostly men who abused it. Women with children to support were not as likely to abuse heroin. If their men became addicted, the women (mothers, aunts, and grandmothers) managed to keep the family going.

Crack cocaine changed all that. Crack is cheap, easy to use, reasonably accessible, and highly addictive. More people, both men and women, are using it. When mothers are addicted families are so much more likely to fall apart.

If you're hooked on crack, you can't take care of your kids. All you think about is how to get more crack. Parents addicted to crack drop out of their families. Drugs send some people to prison, some to mental hospitals, and some on permanent vacations from their responsibilities.

Single parenthood is also changing the family.
Teenage pregnancies have always occurred, but
they have greatly increased in recent years. Recent
statistics say that every year over one million
teenage girls give birth. In addition, teen parents
often got married in the past. That happens less
often today. Teens are starting families before they
have even finished growing up.

Some teens who get pregnant do so intentionally.
Some boys consider it a sign of manhood to father a
child. For a teenage girl, having a baby may be a
way of feeling important and loved. Supporting and
raising the baby is another story, however. When
the newness wears off, many young people can lose
interest in the child. Responsibility often then falls
to other relatives or the state.

Divorce is more acceptable today. People have
come to accept that 50 percent of couples who
marry will break up. And if more parents break up,
who raises the children? With two parents, there's
always one to lean on.

The economy has also changed the picture for the
family. In most families, both parents must work to
make enough money. When Mom's working, she's not
at home taking care of the kids. And if Dad isn't
home either, *who is*?

Unemployment is still another occurrence that
continues to disrupt the family. Moving around in
search of a job uproots whole families. Sometimes
the children don't want to leave. What happens if

people can't find work? How do they support their families?

The stresses of modern society are perhaps greater than in the past. Your grandparents didn't have to worry about guns in schools or drug deals going down in the bathrooms or on street corners. Your generation is faced with all kinds of violence that it can't escape from.

The family is supposed to be a refuge from all these stresses. But the family is part of society and is affected.

Fortunately, even as today's problems overload the modern family, a safety net exists for teens: your relatives.

Why You Might Live with Relatives

The most obvious reason a child lives with grandparents or other relatives is that both the parents have died. Or if one parent dies, the other may not feel capable of raising the children. Relatives may also choose to raise a child who has been abused or neglected by the parents.

Suppose your father got a job in another city and announced that you were moving next month. But you had only half a year before high school graduation, and you didn't want to go. Could you live with Aunt Helen for that six months?

You might end up living with a relative if your

One of the most common reasons to live with relatives is because your parents have died.

parents were committed to a drug treatment center, a hospital, or a jail.

Perhaps your parents are divorced, and neither is able to raise you, so they send you to live with Grandma.

Or you may not be able to get along with your parents. It happens. You might be able to work out the problems in the long run, but in the meantime, it's best to live with relatives. The same is true of trying to get along with new stepparents. Sometimes it helps to take a break from the situation and move in with relatives.

The point to remember is that *it's not your fault* if you have to live with relatives. It doesn't mean you're a bad person or that you're not wanted. You didn't create your parents' shortcomings, or the accident that may have injured them. You, like all children, are supposed to be nurtured to adulthood. It's just that sometimes your parents can't do it for you . . . and that's where your relatives come in.

Chapter 2

Living with Relatives

*A*ngie missed three days of school one week. *She wasn't sick. She had a black eye. How could she explain that to her teacher?*

She could say she had fallen down the stairs. She could say her brother had hit her. She could say she had walked into a door when she got up during the night. But she'd already used those excuses. The truth was that her mother had hit her again. Whenever she got mad, whenever she got drunk, her mother took it out on Angie.

Angie didn't want to get her mother in trouble. It wasn't that she liked things the way they were. She wished her mother wouldn't drink. But if she told anyone what really went on at home, her mother would just hit her again. It never occurred to Angie that she didn't have to live like that . . .

After several more absences and bruises, Angie's teachers called the Department of Human Services.

When you move in with relatives you may be forced to follow rules that are different from what you are used to.

A counselor questioned Angie about the bruises.

"Oh, I fell over one of my brother's toys," Angie said.

"Angie, we're worried that you're getting hurt at home," the counselor said.

"Well, I'm okay."

"You've fallen an awful lot lately," the counselor continued.

"I guess I'm clumsy."

"Well, I'm worried that someone's hitting you."

"No one's hitting me," Angie said, looking at the floor.

"Do you have any other relatives you could stay with?"

"What for?" Angie asked.

"If you're getting hurt at home, you might be better off living with your grandparents or an aunt."

Angie hadn't realized that she could live with a relative. She had figured that if she said anything, the social workers would put her in a foster home. And put her mother in jail . . .

"I don't know if Grandma would want me," Angie said. "And besides, she'd be pretty mad if I said bad things about Mom."

"It's not your fault your mother hits you," the counselor said. "It's not your fault if you have to live with your grandmother. If anyone's at fault, it's your mother. Parents aren't allowed to hit their kids."

Angie wasn't totally convinced, but at least she was talking about the things that were really going on in her home.

When you move in with a relative, you usually encounter a lot of changes, even if you stay in the same town. First, you're in a different house, maybe smaller than you're used to. You might have to share a bedroom (with a more popular cousin, or a squally baby?). You might not even have a room—maybe just a couch.

If you move any distance, you'll probably have to change schools. That means getting used to new teachers, new classmates, different clubs, and a different school atmosphere.

Maybe you'll move out of town. Your new town may be larger or smaller than the one you left. If

You may have to change schools when you move in with relatives.

it's far enough away, you may even have to adjust to a different climate.

But the greatest changes come from living with different people and different rules. Maybe you were the oldest in your family. Now you find yourself the middle child. Or the baby. Maybe you'll be expected to help out with baby-sitting.

Some of you are living with grandparents. No doubt you've clashed on a few rules. They're two generations removed from kids today, and their ideas may seem old-fashioned.

Even though you're closely related, you may have little in common. Maybe you've never set foot inside a church, but Aunt Mary wants you to go to services twice a week. Maybe you were raised a Catholic, but Grandma is Jewish and expects you to be Jewish, too. Are you supposed to make yourself over to fit into this family?

Feelings About Changes

Feelings exist no matter what they are. You can't bury the bad ones and think that's the end of them. They're still hanging around, even if you don't want to recognize them. Sometimes it's enough just to admit that you have bad feelings. Acting out bad thoughts by hurting someone is wrong, but simply thinking bad thoughts is not. It will help you to talk with someone you trust.

Some of you may feel that you're "in the way," or feel guilty that you're imposing on your relatives. It's hard to try to fit in with relatives when you spend most of your time staying out of their way.

Some of you are probably angry. Angry at your parents for not being there, angry at these relatives for rescuing you. Even if your life is better now, it's hard not to be a little bit angry if you think you're supposed to act grateful every minute of the day.

If you're living with grandparents, you might be worried about their health. If something happened to them, what would happen to you?

You might even be embarrassed about the relatives you're living with. Perhaps they see things differently, or act so strangely that they draw attention to themselves. And to you, because you're living with them . . .

You may feel sad because your grandparents act more like parents than grandparents. You have to adjust to this new relationship and recognize why this change has occurred.

If you live with relatives who have kids of their own, maybe you feel jealous of the "real" kids.

Some of you may simply feel resigned. "I can't do anything about it; I've just got to live with it," you think. Or maybe you aren't aware of any feelings one way or the other. That's called apathy. Apathy usually covers up feelings of anger, hurt, or fear. By trying to bury the bad feelings, you end up with literally nothing in their place.

Almost everyone feels a little homesick sometimes, even for the worst of homes. Teens get homesick for the people they love (and it's possible to love people who are mean to you). Sometimes they're homesick for "the way things were." Maybe you'll even start thinking about going back . . .

Just don't lose sight of the positive feelings you have, such as relief that you're in a safe and protected environment and that you have relatives who love you.

Making the Adjusting Easier

Did you ever watch trees in a windstorm? Those

Some teens may attempt to hide their feelings by trying substances like tobacco, drugs, or alcohol.

Going to a new school can be difficult at best, but give yourself a chance.

that bend with the wind spring back. Those too rigid to bend simply break. Keep that in mind as you face these changes. You're like that tree in the windstorm. Being flexible means bending with the wind.

What bothers you most about your new home? Sharing a room? Try dividing the room so that everyone has some part to call his own, even if it's only a corner. Agree on ways to respect each other's privacy. Kids tend to stick to the rules if they help to make those rules.

What if you sleep on the couch? Again, find a living space (even a closet) that you can call your own. Everyone needs some private space.

If you transfer to another school, try to keep things as much the same as possible. That means sticking with the same courses. Join the same clubs or try out for sports that you played before. By getting involved in school activities, you'll carve a place for yourself more quickly.

And involve your relatives in your activities. Grandparents aren't all so old that they can't go to your games. Maybe they don't know you want them to come. So, tell them. Or better yet, ask them.

Give the new school a chance. If you heard bad things about it, maybe the kids who told you the gossip weren't from that school. Let yourself fit in; make new friends. After all, you have enough to deal with outside of school.

If you have moved to a new town, try exploring

it before you turn yourself off to it. You'll probably find something you'll like, even if it's not in your own backyard. Like the tree in the storm, you can't escape the wind. So you adapt to it, and bend, bend, bend.

It takes more work to adjust to new people and new rules. If grandparents are stricter than you'd like, do two things. First, talk to them about the kinds of rules you've had before (and how well they've worked). Be prepared to listen, too. If you understand how they see things, you'll know better how to offer a compromise. Second, work with them on a compromise. If they're against dating, maybe you can have a first date at the house, with them present. Let them see that you are acting responsibly.

And remember, when grandparents take over as parents, they're not going to behave like doting grandparents any longer. They'll act like caring parents, but parents nonetheless.

Keep the lines of communication open. Talk about the things that bother you, as long as they are things that can be changed. If you can't seem to get through to your relatives, ask another adult to help. Maybe a trusted teacher, your minister, or your soccer coach could say something on your behalf without offending your relative. Don't resign yourself to making all the changes. Sometimes grandparents have to do some bending, too.

What about church? Families don't always share

You may find yourself disagreeing with your grandparents about your beliefs or ideas.

religious beliefs. If you never went to church and your grandmother wants you to go with her, give it a try. Churches are good sources of support, not to mention places to meet other teens. Many people find the prayers and music comforting.

What if your ideas differ? Maybe you've attended a radically different church. First, see if another adult from your church can take you to services. Or check out your grandmother's church, if you must. But tell her what you prefer about yours. If your church is an important part of your identity, you don't want to give it up. The more changes you have to adapt to, the greater your stress.

Sometimes the patience and kindness offered by a grandparent or relative is worth the difficulty of adjusting to your new situation.

Finally, try looking at your grandparents in a different light. Sure, they're a couple of generations removed from the present. They may not know what goes on in school these days. But they've been around a long time, and you can learn from them. Maybe not new math or computer skills, but things that don't change with time—things such as patience, kindness, and responsibility.

What to Do When You're Not Adjusting

The more traumatic the circumstances leading

to your move, the greater the stress. Likewise, the greater the changes, the more time you'll need to adjust to them. There's no real timetable. Some teens adjust in a matter of weeks; most adjust in months.

It's normal to feel angry, jealous, guilty, and sad. In time, and as the winds stop buffeting you, you'll bounce back.

But some teenagers become depressed when facing overwhelming stress. Here are some signs to watch out for:

- Doing poorly in school when you've always done well.
- Isolating yourself.
- Having trouble concentrating, following directions, reading books or magazines.
- Changes in sleep habits: sleeping more than usual, or not being able to sleep through the night.
- Changes in appetite: eating everything you can get your hands on, or not feeling hungry at all.
- Loss of energy even before you've exerted yourself.
- Not caring about your appearance anymore.
- Thinking the same thought over and over again.

If you've experienced any of the above signs for more than two weeks, you need help with your

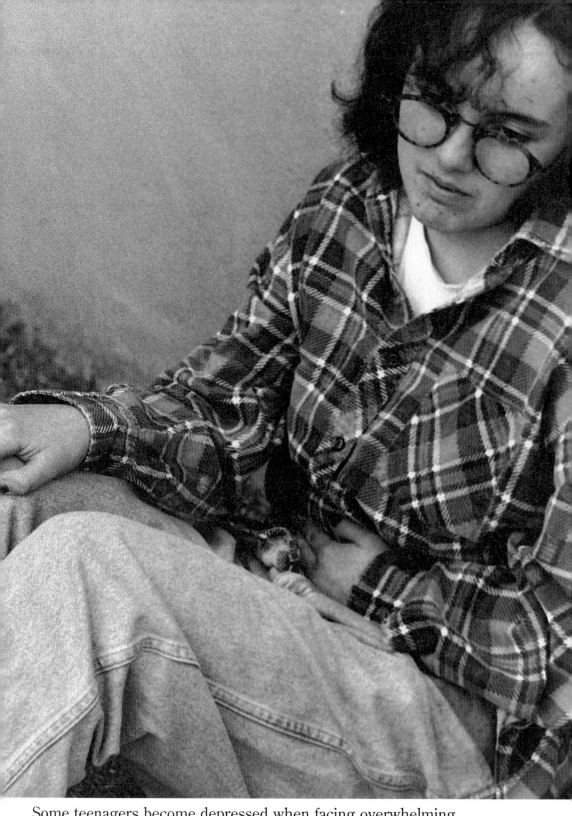

Some teenagers become depressed when facing overwhelming stress.

depression. You can't just will yourself to get better, and no one can get you to "snap out of it." Tell your relative how you're feeling. If he or she doesn't know how to help, ask your school guidance counselor to recommend a mental health counselor. (This is a professional who works with stressed teenagers.) Or make an appointment yourself. Mental health counselors (sometimes called clinical social workers or psychologists) are listed in the phone book. Look them up in the Yellow Pages under Marriage and Family Counseling or Mental Health. Most will give you a first appointment free of charge. You can work out the fee later.

If you're having suicidal thoughts, call a suicide hotline; it's in your phone book, often on the inside cover. Often, what seems overwhelming can be solved by talking it out.

Don't try to solve your problems by using drugs or alcohol; they only cover the problems up.

You can bounce back like the tree in the windstorm. But sometimes you need an outside line to pull you back.

Chapter 3

Worrying About Your Parents

W hen Tony was 11, his mother sent him to live with his grandparents. He thought he was going for the weekend, but the weekend turned into a week, then months, and finally two whole years. He seldom heard from his mother. She only called every other month to check up on him and to tell him she loved him. Well, that was getting harder and harder for him to believe.

His grandmother told him that his mother needed some time to "get herself pulled together."

"What's that mean?" he asked. "And why can't she do it with me around? I could help."

"Well, it's just that she's not very responsible," his grandmother confessed. "She thinks we can take better care of you."

"That just means she doesn't care about me enough," he said.

"I'm sure she loves you in her own way," his

It can be more difficult to live with your parents than with your grandparents or other relatives.

grandmother said. "But she's having problems right now."

Tony really didn't mind living with his grandparents. They were just like parents. They joined his school's PTA; they came to all his games; they let him know that they cared. But he couldn't help wondering what his mother was doing and if she'd ever want him back.

A few weeks before Christmas, his mother showed up. "Pack your stuff," she said. "I'm getting married, and you're going to live with us."

Tony was thrilled that his mother had come back for him. Sure, she had left him for two years, but at least she had come back. He packed his gear, waved

Helping out with jobs like the weekly shoppping can be a great way to feel more comfortable with your new home life.

goodbye to his grandparents, and climbed into her old station wagon.

Three months later, Tony was back. "I can't stand that guy she married," he told his grandfather. "He orders her around, and he tells me to get lost. They don't need me there. And anyway, she's mad all the time."

"Well, maybe you just need to get used to living with your mom again . . ."

Tony slumped down on the couch. "Grampa, I'm so tired of having to get used to stuff," he said.

Depending on your circumstances, you may be feeling sad, angry, relieved, or just plain worried not to be with your parent. Some of you have had to act more like parents than kids, and you may still be worried for your folks now. If your parent is in jail or in the hospital, you may be more worried about him or her than about yourself. Even if your parent hasn't acted much like a parent, you can still care about him. If he's in a treatment facility (or even in prison), you know he's being taken care of, and you can always hope that he'll change for the better.

Worrying night and day about your parent will make it that much harder for you to adjust to your new circumstances. Rather than tell yourself that you don't really care, why not share your fears with your relatives? No doubt they're worried, too. They may not be able to tell you that everything will be fine, but at least they may share some of your worries. You won't feel as if you have to do it all yourself.

Even if your parents were mean to you, even if they ignored you most of the time, you probably still miss them. They *are* your parents. It's okay to be sad. It's okay to miss them.

It's also okay to be mad at them. After all, they didn't take such good care of you. And it's not your fault that they weren't better parents. When people suffer a loss, they go through stages trying to deal with it. They often start out denying the pain. They may then get angry when they accept the truth, and then turn that anger against themselves. "If only I'd done this, if only I'd done that. . . ." If they look past the anger, they'll see that anger often covers up hurt. What many people hate most is the sadness. Getting past the sadness takes time.

You may feel relieved to be in a safer setting, like Jon in Chapter 1 who was relieved to be moving in with his Aunt Paula. But it's hard to feel good about something like this. So, along with the "relieved" feelings, you may also feel guilty.

Guilt may make you behave just the opposite of the way you really feel. For example, you are really mad at your parents. You tell Grandma how you feel, and she says, "I don't blame you. Your mother's been an alcoholic for years. She can't seem to do anything right."

So you say, "Oh, she wasn't so bad. She had her good moments."

Now, do you feel better? Or are you mad at yourself for pretending she wasn't so bad? And mad at your grandmother because she got you to stick up for your mother?

You can't do a lot about changing feelings, but it's always helpful to get them out in the open. Sometimes it helps just to understand *why* you feel a certain way, or that it's okay to feel that way. As was mentioned in Chapter 2, if your behavior changes for the worse because of your feelings, talk to a concerned adult who can recommend someone to help you.

You may feel angry or disappointed with your parent.

It is okay to maintain contact with your parents even though you are living with someone else.

Keeping in Contact

You may be living with grandparents only because a job transfer took your parents away. Your parents are still closely involved; they're just in another city or state. Sometimes that makes for even bigger problems. Who keeps tabs on your schoolwork? Who sets your curfew? Is it Grandma, or Mom and Dad (even though Mom and Dad aren't around)? If you're in this situation, make sure you know who is taking the parental role. No doubt you'll wonder sometimes if this living arrangement is a blessing or a headache. About the best thing you can do is keep the lines of communication open. When problems crop up, at least you'll be able to talk about them.

In the case of divorce, you may be living with your grandparents simply because neither of your parents has the resources to raise you. Maybe you still see your parents on weekends or holidays. Do you feel caught in the middle? Not just between grandparent and parent, but between mother and father? Try not to take sides at all. Let your relatives (including your parents) know that it's awfully hard being in the middle.

Probably the hardest thing to get used to is bouncing back and forth between parents and relatives. How can you adjust to living with relatives when your parents keep popping back into your life?

In the beginning, you'll probably be happy to go

back to them. When teens return to their parents, they usually think things are going to be different. They go back hoping to live like other kids. But when things don't pan out, they're angry all over again. They've had their hopes raised, only to be disappointed again.

Unfortunately, there's not a lot you can do about this situation. You may want to give your parents a second chance, or you might decide that living with a relative is wiser. But in the end, unless the courts intervene, you may not have much voice in the matter. The best thing you can do is talk with a concerned adult about your feelings. It's not fair to be bounced back and forth, never having a really secure home.

Visitation Rights

Even if your parents lose custody of you (because of abuse or neglect), they may still be permitted to visit you. How you handle the visits probably has a lot to do with how you felt about being abused. If you miss your parents or feel sorry for them, you may still want to see them. During the visits, you can see for yourself how your parents are doing. If you've been worried about them, it'll be a relief to know they're doing okay. If the visits upset you, you can cut them short.

Just remember that it's possible to expect too

It can be difficult to see happy families when you are living in a different kind of situation.

much from visits. Situations don't change over-
night, and neither will your parents. You could be
so mixed up about seeing your parents that you
act the opposite of the way you mean to act. You
might really be glad to see them, but act mean and
angry instead. Give yourself and your parents time
to get used to each other.

   If you're afraid of your parents, or still angry,
you may not want visits (even if they're super-
vised). Can the courts force you to see your
parents? Legally the courts can require your
relatives to let your parents visit you, but most
counselors agree that it is not a good idea.

   If you don't want to spend time with your
parents, it's okay not to. Maybe you need more
time to feel better about seeing them. Maybe you'll
never want to see them. If you can't talk to them
about this, write them a letter describing your
feelings. Ask them to leave you alone for a while,
or to write you letters instead. Then you can
reconsider how you feel about them.

   In the opposite situation, you can't force your
parents to come to see you. Waiting for them to
"drop by" keeps your life on hold. Get involved
with other things and other people. Above all,
remember that your parents' seeming rejection
has more to do with *them* than it does with *you*.

Grieving

If your parents have died, you know they're not

Getting involved in some kind of activity helps you keep your life in perspective.

Sometimes writing to your parents helps you share your thoughts and feelings about what's happening in your life.

coming back for you after a while. They're gone. And even if they weren't the best parents in the world, you'll still grieve.

You'll go through the stages of mourning— denial, anger, and sadness—before you accept that they're gone. If they were mean to you, you may feel relieved as well as sad. It's okay to feel both. You can't help your feelings, and pretending not to have those feelings won't make them go away.

If your parents were the world's best, you're still going to be angry. It may not seem to make sense: They didn't mean to die and leave you. But they did, and it's okay to be angry about it. After a while, you'll realize that you're also sad (because you miss them), but relieved to be with loving relatives. These suggestions might speed the process:

1. Talk about your feelings with your relatives. Sharing memories will bring you all closer and help to fill the emptiness.
2. Keep a journal of your feelings. When you look back on them, you'll be surprised to discover that you've gotten better.
3. Stay active. Use your anger's energy in a positive way. Take up a sport; support a cause. Don't get stuck with your grief and anger.

Forgiving Absent Parents

Why bother forgiving parents who abused or

You will go through different stages of mourning before you accept
that your parents are gone.

neglected you? Why not just stay away from them?

Well, forgiveness is a way to let go of your anger. When you're angry, you're still emotionally tied into that relationship and are preventing yourself from moving on. Forgiveness doesn't mean you approve of how they treated you. It simply means that you recognize what they did and then let go of it. And if you want to get on with your life, you can't allow yourself to be full of hatred.

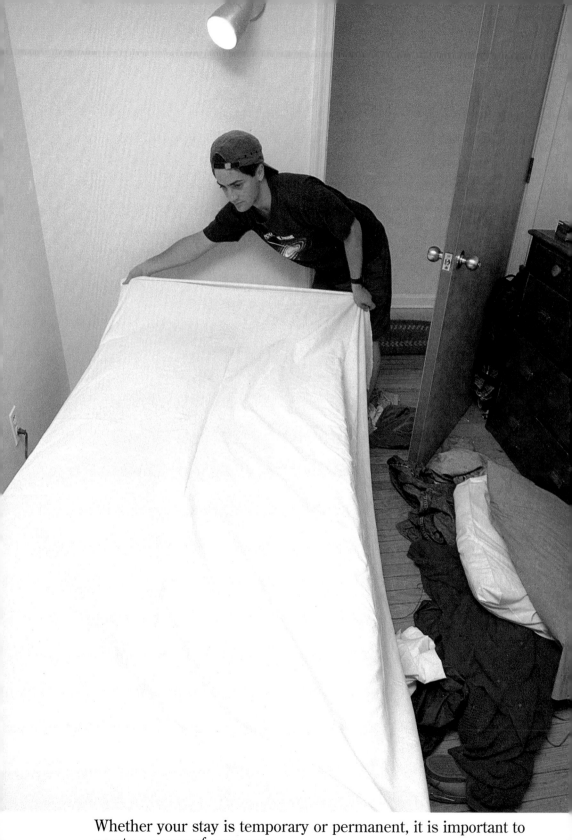

Whether your stay is temporary or permanent, it is important to create a space of your own.

Chapter 4

When Relatives Seek Guardianship

If your parents have abused or neglected you, and it is reported, the Department of Human Services will step in. After the courts have looked into it, they may decide that you should live with a relative. But you may remain in the custody of the state.

What happens more often, however, is that concerned relatives (for example, your grandparents) talk to your parent and offer to have you live with them. Even if your parent agrees, your grandparents need a power of attorney. They would have a lawyer draw up an agreement between them and your parent. Your mother would give your grandparents permission to talk with school authorities about you, or have you treated in a hospital should the need arise. But they would not be your legal guardians. Only through court action could they gain legal guardianship.

Sometimes the confusion and chaos in your life can get you down.

Penny's mother was an alcoholic. Her father was serving time in prison for various drug offenses. When her mother agreed to seek treatment for her drinking problem at a rehabilitation center, Penny went to live with her grandparents. They obtained a power of attorney over Penny, and she lived with them off and on for the next ten years.

Over the years Penny's mother popped in and out of her life but never really wanted her back. As time passed, Penny developed a drinking problem herself. She was too young to sign herself into a rehab center, so her grandparents took her.

"Are you her legal guardians?" the admission clerk asked the grandparents.

"No, but we have power of attorney," they said.

"Who's the legal guardian?" asked the clerk.

"Well, her mother, I suppose," the grandfather said.

"Then either you have to get guardianship or she needs to sign her daughter in."

Fortunately, Penny's mother agreed to sign Penny into the center. But because the mother was the legal guardian, all discharge arrangements had to be checked out with her.

Why didn't the grandparents seek guardianship then and there? For one thing, it's expensive. You have to hire an attorney and go before a judge (which also makes it a hassle). Then, if the parent won't agree to give up her rights, a battle ensues.

Sometimes it may feel as though you have no one to turn to.

So if a teen is close to legal age, many relatives don't push for guardianship (or adoption, which is one step beyond that).

The Legal Process

If a relative wants physical custody of you, a verbal agreement with your parents is not enough. The relative must obtain a power of attorney, which means that your parents have to agree. The agreement is signed in a lawyer's office for a small fee.

If the relative wants guardianship, it's a costlier process. An attorney has to go to district court (even if your parents agree to the arrangement), and a judge decides the matter. If your parents refuse, however, your relative has to prove that your parents are unfit. A judge still decides the case, but Human Services social workers are called in to investigate all people involved.

If the state has reason to believe you're being abused, it assumes custody, although you can still be placed with a relative.

During the court sessions, you could be called to testify about your parents' behavior. It depends on your age and your credibility. Most lawyers (and parents) would rather not put you in that spot. But if they do, remember that you're only testifying to your parents' behavior. They're still the ones who have done something wrong. Telling the court about it doesn't make you guilty of anything.

Adoption is a final step, and most relatives don't seek it. Guardianship serves a similar purpose, except that it can always be challenged by your parents. In adoption, the judge cuts all ties with your biological parents, and your relatives become your legal parents.

Making your living arrangements more secure (either through guardianship or adoption) can take a toll on your emotions. Again, you may feel happy, sad, confused, and anxious. If you have to testify against your parents, you may feel disloyal, or angry with the courts and the lawyers. Talk

The best environment to live in is one in which you are loved and well taken care of, whether it is with your parents or someone else.

with a concerned adult, who can help you deal with your feelings or refer you to a professional. Most lawyers will protect you from testifying if possible, or try to make the experience as easy as possible.

Your parents are not likely to resist your going to stay with relatives. And if the courts do get involved, they probably won't call on you. Most judges want you to get on with your life. If it can't be with your parents, they'll probably want it to be with the relatives who love you.

Chapter 5

Being Abused or Neglected Again

*S*helley *thought her nightmare was over when she moved in with her aunt and uncle. She'd been living with her mother and her mother's alcoholic boyfriend. If the boyfriend wasn't beating her mother, he was yelling at Shelley. Finally a neighbor called Child Protective Services, and Shelley was removed from the home.*

Life with her aunt and uncle was much calmer at first. Then her 15-year-old cousin, Jack, started sneaking into her room at night. He said he wanted to talk, but she didn't like having him sit on the side of her bed. She considered telling her aunt, but what would she say? Jack hadn't really done anything. Yet.

And what if her aunt didn't believe her? What if she thought Shelley was just trying to stir things up?

Not wanting to cause trouble, Shelley packed some things and ran away. She figured that would be

Abuse in any form is not acceptable.

easier—until she started looking for a place to spend the night.

Let's say you've moved in with your relatives, and your parents are no longer involved with you. Just as you're starting to feel comfortable, your uncle (or grandfather) starts acting a little too friendly. Maybe he hugs you in ways that remind you of a boyfriend. Maybe he pats you on the backside when he walks by you. Whatever the case, if you feel uncomfortable, tell someone. First of all, tell the person who's touching you to stop, that you don't like it. If you're scared to tell your aunt or grandmother, tell someone at school or church. They will know how to help you.

If you just can't tell anyone face to face about what's happening, call a crisis hotline. The local number is listed on the inside front cover of most phone books. The national crisis hotline is 1-800-422-4453. This is a free call.

What Is Abuse?

Sexual abuse is everything from sexy remarks that make you feel uncomfortable to someone's touching you where he or she shouldn't. It can progress to sexual intercourse.

Physical abuse is everything from shaking you till your ears ring to beating you black and blue. Anytime "discipline" leaves marks on your skin, that's abuse.

Verbal abuse is harder to define, but its damage is sometimes greater because the scars are not visible. Verbal abuse is everything from nasty remarks that put you down to threats and curses. Children who hear bad things about themselves start to believe them and feel guilty for no cause.

What Is Neglect?

Neglect is also hard to define. Any adult who is caring for you must provide for your well-being. That means feeding you, sheltering you, and keeping you safe. If your relatives leave you alone

Whether you become emancipated, live with your relatives, or move back in with your parents, you are in control of how you deal with what is happening.

(or in charge of younger siblings) with no food or the heating bill unpaid, that's neglect. If your relative is mentally unstable or on drugs, that's also neglect. If you're sick, and you're not taken to the doctor or given medicine, that's neglect. If your aunt knows your uncle is hitting you, and she does nothing to stop it, that's a form of neglect.

If you think your parent or relative is neglecting you, get help. Tell an adult (even a friend's mother), who will contact Child Protective Services. This agency will investigate the matter to see that you're safe.

One word of caution, though. Investigating your family is a serious matter. Even if no wrong-doing is discovered, people in the community will always wonder. Don't report on any family member "just to get back at them." That's like crying wolf. Someday you may really need Child Protective Services to take you seriously.

Emancipation

If you can't live with your parents, and you don't like living with anyone else, is there anything else you can do? If you're 17, you might be able to have a judge declare you emancipated, which means declare you an adult. Gaining emancipation is not easy, though.

For one thing, the rules vary not only from state to state, but county to county. Some juvenile court judges refuse to emancipate teenagers under 18. Other judges will consider it if the child can provide for his or her own basic needs. They require evidence, however. Does the child have a job and a suitable place to stay, and is he or she leading a decent life?

If you're interested in becoming emancipated, call the juvenile court in your county to determine what you need to do. Then get a lawyer to represent you. If you don't have much money, you can consult Legal Aid. They are listed in the telephone book.

Glossary

attorney Lawyer; someone who represents you in court.

Child Protective Services The branch of the Human Services Department that investigates abuse or neglect.

district court Court where guardianship and adoption procedures take place.

emancipation Legal process whereby a teenager is declared an adult.

guardianship Legal process by which an adult other than the parent gains certain rights and responsibilities over the child in his care.

juvenile court Court where emancipation procedures take place.

nuclear family Original family members, consisting of father, mother, and their children.

power of attorney Legal agreement between parent and relative giving the relative authority to have the child treated medically as needed.

rehabilitation center Treatment facility for drug or alcohol problems.

state custody The state acts as legal guardian.

visitation rights Court-authorized arrangement for a parent to visit a child; after divorce, for instance.

Where to Go For Help

In the United States
Alcoholics Anonymous (AA)
P.O. Box 459
Grand Central Station
New York, NY 10163

Big Brothers or Big Sisters of America
220 Suburban Station Building
Philadelphia, PA 19106

Child Abuse Prevention Information Resources Center
1 (800) 342-7472

Families Anonymous
14553 Delano Street
Van Nuys, CA 91411

Family Resource Center
P.O. Box 500
Chisago City, MN 55013
(612) 462-9121

Youth Crisis & Runaway Hotline
(24 hrs)
1 (800) 448-4663

In Canada
Family and Community Support Services Association of Alberta
4732-91 Avenue, 2nd Floor
Edmonton, AB T6B 2L1

Family Service Association of Metropolitan Toronto
22 Wellesley Street E.
Toronto, ON M4Y 1G3

Alcohol and Drug Dependency Information and Counseling Services (ADDICS)
#2, 2471 1/2 Portage Avenue
Winnepig, MB R3J 0N6
204-831-1999

Narcotics Anonymous
P.O. Box 7500
Station A
Toronto, ON M5W 1P9
416-691-9519

Alcoholics Anonymous
#502, Intergroup Office
234 Enlington Avenue E.
Toronto, ON M4P 1K5
416-487-5591

For Further Reading

Aldrich, Robert, and Austin, Glenn. *Grandparenting for the Nineties*. Incline Village, NV: R. Erdmann Publishing, 1991.

Elkind, David. *Grandparenting*. Glenview, IL: Scott Foresman and Co., 1990.

Fontana, Vincent, and Moolman, Valerie. *Save the Family, Save the Child*. New York: Penguin Books USA, 1991.

Forsyth, Sondra, and Kornhaber, Arthur. *Grandparent Power!* New York: Crown, 1994.

Kornhaber, Arthur. *Grandparents, Grandchildren: The Vital Connection*. Garden City, NY: Anchor Press/Doubleday, 1981.

Kroll, Janet. *Directory of Services for Grandparents Raising Grandchildren*. New York: Brookdale Foundation Group, 1994.

LeShan, Eda. *Grandparents. A Special Kind of Love*. New York: Macmillan, 1984.

———. *When Grownups Drive You Crazy*. New York: Macmillan, 1982.

Teyber, Edward. *Helping Children Cope with Divorce*. New York: Lexington Books, 1992.

Index

About the Author
Carolyn Simpson has worked as a social worker in both Maine and Oklahoma. She currently teaches psychology at Tulsa Junior College and lives on the outskirts of Tulsa with her husband and their three children.

Acknowledgments
Many thanks to the following people for their help in gathering data for this book: Vickie Hemken and her parents, Mr. and Mrs. Richard Hemken of Ponca City, Oklahoma; Helen Chamberlain of Oklahoma City; and Rose Perry of the Bureau of Child Welfare, Tulsa, Oklahoma.

Photo Credits
cover, pp. 6, 21, 28, 29, 36, 44, 46, 48, 57 by Lauren Piperno; pp. 2, 9, 16, 25, 26, 32, 41, 39, 55 by Kim Sonsky; pp. 13, 18, 50 by Michael Brandt; pp. 31, 35 by Yung-Hee Chia; pp. 22, 42 by Marcus Shaffer.